The Fabric of Self

The Fabric of Self

by

John McAfee

Woodland Publications

Credits

Editor: Ginny Ruths, Touchstone Publications

Production Manager: Pamela Jones

Production Assistants: Maria Deelman, Jen Irwin

Cover Design: Gary Haney

Design and Production: Graphics West, Inc., Colorado Springs, Colorado

Printer: Kendall Printing, Greeley, Colorado

Copyright 2001 by Woodland Publications

Associate Publisher: Rogue Amazon Publications

Woodland
Publications

2000 Arapaho Street
Woodland Park, Colorado 80863
EMAIL: support@woodlandpublications.com
WEBSITE: http://www.woodlandpublications.com

ISBN 0-9711569-2-1

Dedication

This book is dedicated to the seed of
beauty within the human condition.

The meditations in this book are primarily excerpts from JM's hiking talks held from April through July of 2001. However, a few of the selections have been extracted from his other books, including "The Secret of the Yamas," "Into the Heart of Truth," and "Beyond the Siddhis."

—The Editors

Author Statement

The words in this book, as with every word I have ever spoken, thought, or committed to paper, are on loan to me from the cultures in which I have lived. As the world appears to me, original thought springs, not from the individual, but from the moving totality of life. As such, I claim no ownership of any part of this book. You are free to copy, alter, excerpt, or claim authorship of whatever follows.

—John McAfee

Contents

Introduction

How we relate to experience—to suffering, love, death, loneliness, and the host of other challenges life presents—defines who we are. Our responses to these challenges are the threads of our lives; they are the warp and weft from which we weave our identities—our selves, our egos.

We are a patchwork of personal idiosyncrasies: our own variations on the themes of ambition, sorrow, anxiety, belief, aspiration, opinion, and all the host of petty vanities with which we clothe ourselves. They are the characteristics of our temperament, the shadings of our character and personality.

From life's challenges, and our responses to them, we create our system of beliefs—our attitudes, values, and principles. These are the supporting threads in the fabric of our personal identity. They form our ideology: our image of what life, and our selves, *should* be like. From these values we structure our rituals and traditions, create our habits and routines. They are the basis of our personal drive. Our ambitions and the measurement of our achievements stem from these values, as do our rationalizations and justifications of failures and limitations.

Our virtues are rooted in these values, and because every virtue creates its own opposite, our vices likewise find a home there. This duality is the source of internal conflict. The struggle to maintain our principles and beliefs—our ideals—is the source of fear and anxiety. We are filled with neuroticisms, concerns, suppressions, and insecurities, and these fears fuel our individual idiosyncrasies. They mold our temperament. They fuel our personal sorrows, griefs, and tears. They are the source of our regrets, our bitterness, and our loneliness. These fears color the fabric of our selves.

It is our response to living—to suffering, loneliness, joy, love, desire, healing—that forms the threads of our being. But our relationships are incomplete, fearful, and self-centered. They are based on division, on the separation between ourselves and the rest of the world: on the concepts of "me" and "not me," of "mine" and "not mine." But in reality we are one. There is no identifiable line between "me" and "not me." The fabric of our selves, which we create from the interweaving of these threads, is a curtain that hides the brilliant light of truth shining within each of us.

The meditations in this book address the common threads of our relationship to the world. Through meditation, our relationships to people, to things, and to ideas can be transformed to coincide harmoniously with truth. Through meditation we can pierce the veil of our self-image. We can come to the source of beauty, to the infinite, timeless state that is immortality.

Awareness

Awareness is the fundamental force of change for the self. When we become aware, deeply and completely, of the attachments, prejudices, arrogance, bitterness, fears, and all the other vanities that make up our daily existence, then true change is realized.

Awareness is the natural result of abandoning illusion. As long as we deny our true natures, struggle against our vices, and attempt to discipline or change the reality of ourselves, then awareness will elude us. When we abandon the struggle and cease our self-judgments, then we banish illusion, and open ourselves to awareness.

To be aware of every thought, every act, every gesture, expression, word, and feeling; and at the same time to be aware of the wind rustling through the trees, and of the sun reflecting from the damp rocks, and of the person sitting next to you: This is what it means to be fully here, in the moment. This place, right here, right now, is where the truth lies. It is always here, always moving, always living.

How can we be aware in the present moment when we are rehashing a past experience or planning some future event, or chewing over some insult or flattery? And what is our level of awareness when we are judging the present moment: comparing, evaluating, scheming, demanding, or rejecting? We are aware only of an image—a construct used for comparison. The image is not reality. The present is the only reality.

Meditation

Meditation is not something that we do for brief periods, in isolation, with closed eyes, repeating a mantra, or emptying the mind. It is not something that we *do* at all. It is something that *happens* when we drop our judgments and our attempts to control. It is a condition of openness from which we are able to perceive the heart of truth. Meditation happens when we observe without choice and without any wish to change what we observe. It is a state of clarity and purity, without which we cannot come to a complete understanding of ourselves.

We must combine meditation with living. It is easy to find peace in a cave, isolated from the world of temptations and antagonisms, or in a quiet room for a few minutes each day. It is much more difficult to bring that peace into the world of relationships. It is in the world of action, the world of relationships, that meditation has its place and its value.

Meditation is a way of living, not an isolated practice. It is a way of looking at the world. It is complete awareness in all of our actions. It is observation without the observer, thought without the thinker, experience without one who experiences. It is the beginning and the end, the first step and the last.

The question is not how to meditate, but what meditation is. If meditation had a "how," then it would be mechanical, a formula, a finite process; and we cannot encompass the infinite through any finite thing. We wish to know truth, beauty, and immortality. But these things are boundless, alive, moving, and we can only know this movement by breaking down our mechanistic practices and abandoning our formulas. Meditation is meeting each moment of life anew. If we understand this simple thing, then the "how" becomes meaningless.

$\mathcal{T}$here can be no meditation where there is effort or control. Effort and control imply a goal that we wish to achieve. But a goal is necessarily of the future, so our focus has shifted to the future. Thus we use the present as a tool to achieve some future result, and the present becomes a means to an end rather than the end itself. But truth exists eternally in the moment, and meditation is the awareness of that moment.

Love

Without love you are an empty shell. You may work, hope, dream, seek riches and power, but your conflicts and suffering will continue. The absence of love creates an emptiness that cannot be filled by any ambition, success, pleasure, or possession. Fear grows in this emptiness. But where love exists, there is fullness and life.

We have all known the beauty of love, and the possessiveness that follows. This possessiveness leads to jealousy, and then to anger. But can possessiveness, jealousy, and anger co-exist with love? They cannot. The one destroys the other. Love eradicates personal hatreds and jealousies, and jealousy or possessiveness destroys love. True love has no object. It is a state of being. It is the infinite beauty of life that blossoms when we see the pettiness of our jealousy, the futility of our possessiveness, and the root of our anger.

There is no possibility of love while we are pursuing our own demands and desires, our own private pleasures. Love is not pleasure or sensation, and it cannot be found through gratification or self-fulfillment. If we are filled with ambitions and expectations, or are fearful, jealous and envious, then we have no room for love. It is only when the mind is quiet, when we forget our selves, that love can come into being.

We cannot love while we each live in our own world, at every moment concerned with ourselves. When we seek inner security through outward relationship, we are using relationship as a means of escape from loneliness. We depend on another for comfort, companionship, or pleasure. We use one another. This state is not love.

We claim to love, but our love is based on sex or pleasure, personal security or need. We find escape through love, or seek to fill some internal void. For most, love is a means to some end, a way to gain happiness or sustain some ideal. If our love relationships lack true depth, bring jealousy and anger, and offer only limited harmony, then what hope have we for any other relationship?

When we touch the root of love, we find that only one love exists. The romantic love; the love for a child, brother, or parent; the love of God; and the love for mankind are all the same love.

Listening

When we listen to another through the filter of our prejudices, opinions, and beliefs, we are listening only to our own thoughts; we do not truly hear the other. What we hear instead is the image of the other that we have created, and this image is in turn a reflection of our own self-image.

*C*an you listen with your full being? Not simply to words, but to the meaning behind the words? Can you listen without judgment, without censorship or comparison? Can you listen without analysis or classification, without the filter of your ideals and conclusions? If not, then there will be no true communication.

$\mathcal{J}$t is insight into truth, into reality, that frees our minds. However, insight can only occur when we listen, not only to the words of others, but to the meaning behind them. When we listen with complete attention, without preconceived opinions, we perceive the reality beneath words and images. We perceive the true as the true, the false as the false, and the relationship between the true and the false.

If you listen, not just to these words,
but to the birds in the aspen, to the wind as
it gently rustles the leaves, to the stirring of
the person next to you, and to the whisper
of the brook in the distance, and if you hear
all of this as one sound, one movement,
then you are listening with your full being.

The World

We are the world. Not as some warm, fuzzy image, nor as an intellectual concept, but in actuality, in form and substance, in truth. No line separates you from the world. There is no division, no wall. No entity exists to observe the "not me" from a position of separateness. Your very consciousness, your thoughts, your ambitions, your values, your striving—all of these are the world. You are the world and the world is you. It is an inescapable fact, a tangible reality.

We have created this world. It is a reflection of each of us. As we are petty, narrow, and bigoted, so are our institutions, religions, states, and national groups. How could it be otherwise? Our institutions are made up of individuals. The collective does not exist apart from the individual. And as the individual is, so is the collective, only magnified by the number of people that comprise it.

We have each of us created this world. There are no exceptions. And the world in turn has created us. We are the result of all of the world's past conflicts, its past corruptions. The society created by our parents and grandparents is the society in which we live. Our driving forces—fear, pleasure, desire, and ambition—are common to all mankind. We may express them through individual idiosyncrasies, and they may be colored by our culture, religion, and ethnicity, but we cannot claim separateness.

We have created a world of conflict through our self-centered activities, and that world of conflict, in turn, has created self-centeredness in the individual. It is an unending circle. Our relationship to the world will continue to be one of conflict and illusion as long as we relate from our center of selfishness.

We live in the world of people, the society of mankind. It is the world of business, politics, industry, and social and economic striving. It is a world divided into competing nations, cultures, races, religions, and ethnic groups. It is a world filled with ambition and possessiveness, antagonisms and hatreds. It is a world of increasing knowledge and decreasing harmony. We cannot relate to this world in any sane manner while we are, at the same time, adding our own petty ambitions and greeds to the disharmony.

Death

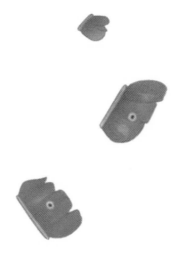

We cannot separate death and beauty; they are intertwined. When we live completely, in the moment, death becomes part of the beauty of life. We die to each moment as it is lived. Life then becomes timeless and infinite; the true meaning of death is revealed. Thus we achieve immortality.

We fear death because we have never fully lived. By fearing death, by denying it, we remove ourselves from the infinite beauty that is living, and fear grows in its stead. We then fear both living and dying.

Death is an ending. It is the ending of the body, of thoughts, of memories. It is the ending of an individual personality with a name, a form, and a list of personal idiosyncrasies. But every ending of one thing is the beginning of something else. It is our identification with the body, with our petty egos, with our thoughts and memories, that causes distress in the face of death. In truth we are the world, and it is the life of the world with which we should be concerned.

We cling to our egos in the face of death. We search for permanence. We grasp any belief that offers hope of continuance. We are quick to seize reincarnation, after-life, heaven, or any other concept that offers hope for survival after death. But what is this ego that we are attempting to make permanent? It is a bundle of opinions, prejudices, and idiosyncrasies, limited in thought, bound by time, and constrained through past conditioning. It is a petty, finite entity. But when we abandon this entity, in its entirety, the infinite blossoms in its place. Infinity is a thing beyond death and time. In this deathless state, concerns with permanence or continuity do not arise. Infinity is its own answer.

Suffering

*O*ur natural response to suffering is avoidance: when we suffer, we seek comfort, distraction, and relief. Thus we never truly know the depth of suffering. Yet, in the heart of suffering lies the immensity of truth. When we sit with suffering, when we embrace it fully, as the truth of ourselves in that moment, suffering transforms itself. Then our raw loneliness melts into the infinite flowering of life. We wake into a timeless state in which joy and suffering are the same energy.

The source of all suffering is our self-centered possessiveness. We grieve at *our* losses, *our* disappointments, *our* distress. We possess people, things, reputations, knowledge, and talents, and their inevitable loss causes suffering. But our possessive existence is at odds with reality—with the truth that we are the world, that we are not separate. Because we are the world, there is nothing we truly possess, and therefore nothing we can truly lose.

Why is it that we perceive our own suffering as all consuming, while the suffering of millions of others is faint and distant? Surely, the suffering of others is no less than our own. They are no less human, no less vulnerable, no less sensitive. Our suffering swells disproportionately because we are disconnected from life—we are isolated. If we were aware of our connectedness; if we saw, at the deepest level, that we are an inseparable part of mankind; then our own suffering would cease entirely.

Our lives are based on imitation and repetition. We imitate the things we wish to become, and we repeat the words and ideas of others. We are second-hand people. But imitation is not living. When we are fully aware in the moment, we are in beauty and truth; when we imitate, we invite suffering.

Loneliness

Loneliness is the absence of relationship. To be lonely is to have no true relationship with life—with wife or husband, with companions, with nature, with the wind and trees. This lack of relationship is the emptiness in which the despair of loneliness resides.

Loneliness is the awareness of isolation, and we create isolation by building a wall that divides us from the world. It our security against the ravages of life, and it is what separates each of us from the other. Yet it has nothing but emptiness behind it, and we spend our lives trying to fill this emptiness. It is a futile task, for as long as the wall exists we cannot banish the emptiness. This emptiness is the absence of love, and love can only flow when the wall is demolished.

We attempt to escape loneliness through activity. We cultivate hobbies, join groups, attend parties and social events. We fill our days with diversions—movies, sports, play, work—yet in the dark hours of night, or when our entertainments fail us, we see that emptiness is always present. No activity, no social belonging, no amount of family, friends, or lovers will fill the inner void from which loneliness springs. But by boldly entering the heart of emptiness—by tearing down the wall that divides us from the world—loneliness is transformed into infinite joy.

Loneliness results from our quest for security. Security is a self-enclosing process, a process of isolation; we can only be secure by shutting out the world. This process creates emptiness—we have removed the world, removed life, from the core of our being.

Nothing can fill our inner emptiness: not noise, gossip, lust, money, knowledge, rituals, nor any person, thing, or idea. Whatever we may use in the attempt to complete ourselves—to make part of ourselves—we merely isolate ourselves from it. Thus, we seek to bond with others while at the same time building walls to keep them out. We seek to belong, but see ourselves as separate from the groups that we join. We are incapable of taking anything truly into ourselves.

Relationship

Because we have no true, deep relationship with the world, we are unable to see things freely, with joy and without jealousy or greed. We are unable to see people who are happy with their lives, with the things that they have and we do not, and to be happy *with* them. Nor do we have compassion for those who are poor. We envy those with more than ourselves, and we shun those with nothing. If we understood our true relationship with the world, we would see that both the happy and the miserable are in reality ourselves.

*O*ur relationships bring exploitation, because they are instruments of gratification. But true relationship is based on communion, and communion cannot coexist with exploitation. Thus, our relationships are incomplete; they create unending conflict. Our relationships divide instead of joining.

Relationship is society. And we have created a society with a structure based on mutual use, mutual gratification, and acquisitiveness. We have created a world of cruelty, hostility, and war through our relationships, and society is in crisis. But the crisis is not just in the outer world; it is in human consciousness itself. We live in and are conscious only of our own, isolated world, and true relationship eludes us.

All of life is relationship; it is how we relate to people, things, ideas, and our past actions that defines who we are. Our relationship to our possessions causes fear and anxiety, or a sense of security and well being. Our relationship to our ideas—cultural, religious, social, moral—provides a basis for making decisions and judging our progress through life. Our relationship to our past and continuing actions is the source of our pride or shame. But it is our relationship to others that defines us most profoundly—it is the mirror in which we may see ourselves.

All of our actions in life are in relationship to something. There can be no action in the absence of relationship. It is through relationship that we assert our personal identities, and it is in the mirror of relationship that we see ourselves and know our natures.

Ego

The line that separates the self, the ego, from the world is an illusion, a construct, a creation of thought. It has no basis in reality. But to see this with the intellect alone has no value. If we want to change, truly, deeply; if we want to end suffering and ignorance; if we want to know reality, truth, and beauty; then we must grasp, with our whole being, with our hearts and minds, the truth of our relationship to the world.

The ego grows out of our sense of separateness. There is "me" and then there is everything else. The entire world, its billions of people, its commerce, industry and noise, its structures and organizations—all these constitute the "everything else," the "not me." The absurdity of this separateness is the enormous importance we give to the "me;" of the rest of the known universe, we are concerned only with those few elements that enlarge or amuse the "me."

We are consumed with ourselves. We agonize over personal fears or thwarted ambitions, while we watch the deaths and sufferings of countless millions with near indifference. We may utter, "what a pity" or even shed a tear, but we quickly return to our own petty miseries—our lost jobs or dwindling bank accounts. Can we claim to live when we shut out all of life?

The ego is expansive, perpetually seeking to enlarge itself. It is always attempting to become more, greater, better. Regardless of its possessions or securities, it always seeks something beyond—greater talents, better looks, more power, additional knowledge, wisdom, or pleasure. We live a constant quest to achieve some vaguely defined state of perfection or grace. But the ego is unsatisfied except for brief moments here and there that quickly become part of the web of the past.

The substance of the ego—the basic qualities of separateness and expansion—is as inconstant as our thoughts, which wander perpetually from one triviality to another. Can such an entity have any real continuity? Can it become something greater, something more perfect, something other than what it is? Can it exist as a separate entity from the world? On all counts, it cannot.

*O*ur individuality, our consciousness, our ego, is a product of uncountable thoughts extending backwards into the mists of time. The world has handed us a structure of thinking, intact, with which we identify and clothe ourselves. We are given the words, the concepts, the values, and to these we add what pitiful few experiences we have—and that is what we call our self.

Thought

We live in a world of thought, created by thought and maintained by the process of thinking. And we ourselves are a product of thought. Our acquired prejudices, beliefs, manners, and customs were given to us through a legacy of past thoughts handed down through generations. Our concepts of right and wrong, good and bad, have been created and refined by thought through thousands of years of internal struggles. The concepts of ambition, growth, acquisition, and generosity have existed as thoughts for as long as we have recorded time, and these thoughts continue through us. The process of thinking controls all of our actions, choices, and identifications. It is the world of thought that has created divisions, and therefore suffering.

$\mathcal{T}$hought has created our sense of self. We are a product of thinking. Our very consciousness is grounded in the memories of all our past experiences, and this memory is the basis of thinking. We think in words, in images, and these words and images have been acquired in memory through the action of experience. If we are to know ourselves, we must first know our process of thinking.

*T*hought creates conflicting ideologies, and therefore wars and hostility. It creates social structures, customs, and collective habits, and therefore causes cultural separation and prejudice. It created the concept of ownership, which brings all the attendant jealousies. It has created all systems of religion: the dogmas, rituals, practices, and separative beliefs. It is thought that has created all of our concepts and ideas about God, and it is concepts and ideas created by thought that separate us from God, from truth, from reality.

We cannot know truth and reality through thought. Thought is finite, limited by knowledge, and based on memory, which is the repository of the past. Thought seeks permanence, stability, and security. But truth is infinite and cannot be encompassed by words or images. It is moving, alive, ever in a state of revealing itself. In truth there is no security; there is infinity.

Belief

What is belief? It is something fixed, static, frozen—a conclusion we have reached. Once we believe something, we shut the door to everything outside of, or opposed to, that belief and stop enquiring. Belief is our substitute for truth, for awareness. It is what we cling to when we have no true understanding. Only the blind must believe in sunlight. For those who can see, belief plays no part in the experience of seeing.

The various systems of belief throughout the world do nothing to ease mankind's hatreds, prejudices, wars, and animosities. It is belief itself that has created our divisions. It is my belief against yours, my rights and your wrongs, my god over your god. Belief has created competing ideals, dogmas, and rituals. It has created fear and hatred of its opposite. It is responsible for most of our wars and our individual hostilities. To solve any of our personal, or the world's, problems, we must transcend belief. We must see the source of our need for belief and go beyond it.

Belief, in the end, creates formulas and fixed patterns for living. It provides us with ready responses to whatever situation may arise. Thus we are never free to act in the fullness of any moment. Life is infinite in its unfolding; it cannot be met with formulas and scripts. Belief is a tether that keeps us forever in the tiny circle of our vanities.

Belief is the greatest of our vanities. We judge, choose, and reach conclusions, and from these conclusions we create concepts and images. We vest these images with the illusion of reality; we give them life, and they in turn allow us to think that we *know*. But knowing is always of the past. It is fixed, lifeless, immovable. Knowledge is not reality. It is an image that we create of reality, a dead thing.

Joy

Joy is spontaneous. It is the result of meeting each moment in life afresh, with no expectations, preconceptions, or judgments; no desire to cling to, repeat, or capture the moment. Joy happens when we allow life to unfold in its natural course.

Joy and pleasure oppose one another. Joy is unplanned; pleasure is contrived. Joy is uninvited; pleasure is pursued. Joy is of the moment; pleasure requires continuity. In joy, we have no sense of ego; in pleasure, the ego is all that exists.

It is the nature of the ego to transform joy into pleasure. We experience joy when the ego momentarily forgets itself—when we are for a brief moment aware. We see, for example, the exquisite beauty of a rainbow and we lose ourselves in the joy of that beauty. The ego then wants to repeat the experience, to see more rainbows, to have more joy. But the eternal present is in constant motion and there is no "more" of anything. In the quest for "more," we abandon the present and seek gratification in some future moment. We thus abandon joy and begin to desire pleasure, which is always of the future.

We fear fundamental change in ourselves because we are afraid of losing what little we have. If we become compassionate, then we fear we may forget our own possessions, power, and vanities in favor of the needs of the world. Yet, when we see the true nature of our ego and abandon it entirely, then the entire world is ours—we lose nothing. Each moment of existence is joy.

Desire

Desire is a creation of thought. We remember a pleasant experience, and from that memory, thought creates an image of repeating the experience, or a similar one, in the future. The ego seeks continuity through such repetition. This striving for continuity of experience is the source of desire.

Desire is the other face of fear—they are inseparable. Whatever we fear, we desire its opposite: if we fear poverty, we desire riches; if we fear loneliness, we desire companionship. And in the heart of desire lives the fear of not having, or losing, the very thing that we desire.

Desire can never be fulfilled. Whether we desire love, spirituality, power, sex, wisdom, or any other thing, we cannot overcome the insecurity that accompanies the acquisition of desire's object. When we acquire power, we desire more to ensure that no one can take it from us. When we acquire love, we desire assurance that the other's love for us will not wane. When we acquire sex, we desire the repetition of sex. We become obsessed with keeping, and with the fear of losing, whatever we acquire. Thus, desire cannot be fulfilled because the root of desire is fear. Desire will continue, unabated, until fear, in all of its manifestations, is faced and understood.

All desire is for sensation—either the physical sensations of touch, sight or taste, or the sensation provided by thoughts and images. We have the obvious physical desires for sex, food, and bodily pleasures, but we equally desire money, power, prestige, social position, and the love of others. These desires stem from thoughts and the process of creating images. Thus, those who abandon all pleasures and desires, choosing a spiritual path of austerity, still live with unabated desire. They now desire spirituality, and take pleasure in the image of austerity. Only in understanding the root of desire can we transcend desire.

Emotional Hurt

Hurt and flattery are two sides of the same coin. There could be no hurt if we had no need for flattery. We are hurt when our self-image is threatened or disturbed. But our self-image is artificial, inflated, based on ideals and aspirations, and supported by our self-deception. We need constant praise and admiration in order to sustain the image. But when we see ourselves as we truly are—when we give up our self-image and live fully in the present moment—then flattery and insult do not touch us.

Have you ever observed what is hurt when you are insulted? It is certainly not your body. Nor your intellect; your mental capacities remain intact. Your knowledge, sense of humor, charm, talents, and professional capabilities are untouched. What then suffers from the words or implications of another? It is your self-image. But this self-image would not be vulnerable if it were not, at its very core, false.

We hurt because we aspire to be what we are not. We are incomplete and empty, so we seek wholeness and fulfillment. We establish ideals and strive to attain them. When we inevitably fall short, we are hurt. But suffering ends the moment we abandon our efforts to escape from ourselves, the moment we stop aspiring for something more and better.

Hurt is a by-product of vanity. We are self-important, and the image that we have of ourselves is who we believe we are. When the structure of the image collapses—as it must, because it has no foundation in reality—we are crushed. However, when we bring our self-image into line with our true natures, such collapse is impossible, and hurt does not occur.

Gurus

We seek gurus because we want someone else to show us who we are. This notion is an absurdity. We live within the sphere of our vanities—our own lusts, brutalities, habits, attachments, and anxieties. These are all that we know; they are our life. And as long as we are looking to someone, or something else for the truth of ourselves, we cannot look at this sphere of our self—and thus we will never see who we truly are.

The relationship between guru and disciple is one of mutual exploitation. Disciples abandon the difficult task of self-discovery and rely on the guru for understanding, hope, security, peace, wisdom, or whatever else they have been unable to achieve alone. Gurus, in turn, exploit disciples by providing the illusion that they can transmit something of value. But whatever self-understanding gurus may have, they cannot impart it to anyone else. Truth, beauty, reality, the infinite—whatever you may wish to call it—can only be lived. It cannot be given or taught to anyone.

Gurus provide an alternative to facing fear. At the heart of self-inquiry is the perpetual fear of the emptiness of ourselves. If we look to a guru, however, we look outside of ourselves, and thus are spared the fear of true inquiry.

The truth of ourselves can only be seen in our relationship to the present moment—in our thoughts, actions, and feelings as they are happening. That relationship is itself the only meaningful guru. There is no other.

Ideals

We create the ideal because we are divisive, and therefore incomplete. We divide the world into "me" and "not me," and we compare ourselves to the world from which we have thus separated ourselves. We judge, and find ourselves insufficient. So we create the ideal: the thing that we hope to become, the thing that we are not. It is the standard by which we judge the behavior of ourselves and others. The ideal is the false mirror that forever keeps us from seeing the reality of ourselves.

We judge ourselves and others based on our ideals. But what are these ideals? They are images that we have created in our minds, formed from cultural icons, from stories told to us by parents, from legend and fairy tale, from newsreels and magazines, from schooling, and from the inadequacy of our own experience. They are fabrications based on our conclusions of what people *could* or *should* be, or how they *might* behave. They have no basis in reality. Thus, the ideal is in constant conflict with our true natures.

*O*ur self-image consists of a core of ideals: of aspirations and ambitions that mold our opinions and beliefs, our fears and insecurities, our desires and habits. Our entire repertoire of vanities, arrogance, regrets, and hopes resides in this core. But this core of ideals is a dream, an artificial construct. It focuses on the future, on continual improvement through time. It denies the present, and thus truth.

We are marching incessantly toward the ideals that we have created. And each step of this march is a step away from the truth of ourselves. When we abandon the ideal, when we discontinue the march, we are left with our true natures. Only then can lasting change take place.

Time

We have divided life into past, present, and future. The past is composed of memory; the future is the projection of that memory; and the present is the tool that we use to transform the past into the future. We act in the present to achieve some future goal—pleasure, security, or continuity. We attempt to relive the past through the reactivation of our memories, and to create the future through action of the will. The present is lost in this process. Yet neither the past nor the future exists. The present is the only reality.

We structure our actions in the present to maintain our existence in the future. We judge every choice in life on the basis of our continuance. Thus, we secretly approve of greed, possessiveness, and hoarding. We feel sorry for the suffering and misery in much of the world, but are secretly thankful that we are not part of it. We plan and cunningly work toward a future in which we still exist, irrespective of our impact on the world.

The ego is poor, empty, and isolated, and hopes for relief through some future experience. It knows that it is incomplete in the present moment, and that its only hope lies in the future, in different, improved circumstances. So what it cannot live today it will live tomorrow. Thus for the ego, the present is no more than a means of reliving the past and reaching the future.

We are made up of our past experiences—hurts, pleasures, fears, losses, and gains. We are a composite of the past. The self is intricately woven into this fabric of past experiences and responses, and it requires the continued existence of this past in order to continue its own existence. Thus, we create formulas for living and face each new event armed with our past experiences and preconceived courses of action. We never meet life anew.

Violence

Violence is the attempt to impress our will or our beliefs onto others. We do violence to another each time we attempt to sway someone to our point of view, or dissuade someone from a course of action that we, in our arrogance, feel is wrong.

Violence is our response to threats against our security. We have constructed complex walls of relationships, financial arrangements, ideals, and religious beliefs, behind which we hide from change and uncertainty. When these walls are threatened, we respond with some form of subtle or overt violence.

That we possess the ideal of nonviolence is proof that we are violent by nature, for if we were not violent we would have no need for the ideal. Our violence is a fact, as factual as the page on which these words are printed. To see the root of our violence we only need to look.

Violence is rooted in fear, and we are filled with fears and suspicions. We may not openly assault our neighbors or take out our frustrations on innocent bystanders, but our fears nevertheless mold our behavior, and in the heart of whatever passivity we may muster lies the seed of violence.

God

It is easy to love God. God does not trespass on your property, hurl insults while you drive down the street, or flirt with your spouse. Loving your neighbor is far more difficult. Yet, can we truly love God, whatever conception we have of God, if we do not love all people, all creatures, all of creation?

We have created an image of God. Because this image is a creation of thought, it is finite. It cannot touch the reality of God at any point. To touch the infinite we must abandon the finite. We must recognize the creation of images as an illusion.

Religions—the practices, dogmas, separative beliefs, customs, and priestly structures—are a creation of thought, and while thought did not create God, it certainly created all of our concepts, ideas, and images of God. The various images of God have been handed down through generations, colored by social and individual vanities, augmented by fears of death—and life—and clothed in our own individual conceptions, which are based on personal experiences and idiosyncrasies. If God—the infinite, the unbounded—exists, surely we can never know this infinite existence by looking through the distorted image that we have created.

We want to know God, but do not know ourselves. Yet, surely, if God exists, then that existence must be present in each of us. How can we know God if we do not look first into ourselves?

Knowledge

Knowledge is a dead thing. It is memory, which is the past. We need knowledge to do our jobs, drive a car, and find our way home. But can knowledge show us truth, beauty, or the infinite spirit of the present moment? It cannot. The present moment is living, moving—it is ever unfolding. It cannot be "known" in the usual sense of the word. We can have an insight into the reality of the present; we can have an understanding as the present flows, but we cannot *know* this infinite movement. It cannot be placed into memory—cannot be fixed, made static and retrievable. Memory is limited. Reality is infinite.

We turn knowledge into a vanity. It becomes a possession, like our houses, cars, and toys. We delight in displaying the depth of our knowledge in our areas of interest, or we feel shame at our lack of knowledge in comparison to others. This vanity of knowledge becomes our greatest liability when we attempt to understand ourselves. We begin the inquiry into ourselves with the illusion that we *know* certain things about reality, and this knowing clouds our perception. Reality cannot be known. It can only be perceived, and perception must take place without judgment, and without the knowledge in which judgment is grounded.

Whoever says, "I know, and you do not" is living in a divided world—a world of duality. When reality is perceived with your entire being, with your full body and mind, then there is no knowing, no knowledge—only perception.

We thirst for knowledge, but what is this thirst? In reality, it is a thirst for pleasure. The pleasure of knowledge is no different than any other pleasure of the body or mind. There is nothing wrong with knowing, but we must see it for the simple thing that it is. We delude ourselves when we believe that knowledge is equivalent to wisdom or understanding. Knowledge of *things* is memory; it will not show us ourselves.

Healing

We are insecure in our self-image; we must be, because reality cannot support our self-image. Self-image is molded by ideals—by how things might be, by how we should behave and feel—and these ideals are in constant conflict with our true natures. This conflict is an exercise in vanity, resulting in an unreal world in which we live out our sorrowful existence. We cannot heal ourselves until we first heal the fractured image that we have of ourselves.

It is an absolute necessity that we heal the image that we have of ourselves—not partially, in pieces here and there, but completely, in its totality. We must make the image whole. Our self-image must correspond precisely with the reality of ourselves. If we are able do that, then all our images of others will evaporate; we will no longer need to buttress our self-image with artificial images of others. We will relate to people as they are, in their reality, from our own position of reality.

The purpose of self-observation is understanding. We are not observing ourselves so that we can change into something else. We are observing so that we can see the truth of ourselves, in the moment, in the now. That understanding is itself the change. It is the healing.

It is through questioning, with the burning desire to know the answer, that the truth is revealed. And it is ourselves whom we must question. This questioning of ourselves is the only road to a full healing of ourselves.

Will, Choice,
and Freedom

What is the root of will? When we say, "I will do this," or "I will not do this," or "I will become something," what is this will? It is merely the manifestation of desire. It is the tool used by desire for its own fulfillment. The various compulsions of our competing desires make up the threads of our will, with which we attempt to achieve our goals, satisfy our lusts, and become what we are not.

It is mankind's vanity to believe that because we have choice, we are free. But what is choice? It is no more than a thought process based on conditioning. We choose one thing over another based entirely on events and conditions that are out of our control. We choose according to a formula of ideals and competing desires that create a complex web in which we are caught. We choose professions based on all of our past knowledge and conditioning. We choose pleasures based on our structured and predetermined idiosyncrasies. We choose our self-image based on the standards given to us by society. Is this freedom? I say not. Freedom is an unconditioned state, a state in which choice is transformed into action.

The idea of choice has created conflict in our lives. We create concepts of good and bad, right and wrong, mine and not-mine, and based on these comparisons, choice grows. But these concepts exist entirely in the world of thought, in the world of ideals. The process of choosing operates in this field of concepts, not in the actual. In the reality of the living moment, there is only what is.

What do we do when we choose? We first create images of the potential end results of the choice. Then we compare these images using the process of thought. We weigh the results and then choose a course of action. In effect, we have acted in the present based entirely on our anticipated and expected results in the future. We have thus used the present instead of lived it. In freedom there is no process of choosing a future result. Living completely in the present moment brings with it the appropriate action—the action is an integral part of the moment. This is living in fullness.

Choice is possible only when we have divided living into past, present, and future. All choices are based on past knowledge; we use past knowledge to choose a future result. However, the past and the future do not exist. All time is now. If we are living eternally in this now, then choice as we know it ceases. What remains is the movement of this eternal present.

We know many types of freedom. There is the freedom resulting from talent, knowledge, wealth, capacity, or ability. There is the freedom from our own oppressions—from fear, desire, habit, or anger. There is freedom from external oppressions—from political or cultural confinement. There is freedom of the body, and freedom of thought. All these freedoms are sought through will and choice. But a different freedom exists, a freedom that is not *from* anything. It is a state of being—causeless and unconditioned. This freedom cannot be brought about through choice or will. It is something that happens when we go beyond choice and will.

We seek freedom, but freedom will not come until our minds are sensitive to and capable of seeing truth. We must be open, vulnerable, defenseless, for truth is subtle and easily distorted by the coarseness of thought. But when the mind possesses the quality of sensitivity, then truth can enter—the truth of ourselves—and freedom follows.

Discontent is the beginning of freedom. It is the sense that there must be something else, a sense of disillusionment with life that creates a constant searching and inquiring. This search for something to happen, to change, to transform, is the energy that moves us toward freedom. But the energy must flow in its natural course, unimpeded by will and choice.

Authority

Authority creates stagnation. It is a formula with which we meet the mystery of living. Authority gives us our rights and wrongs and thus predetermines our courses of action. It is a chain that ties us to the known, and prevents us from glimpsing the unknown.

We are filled with authority. We have the authority of the state, of the church, of parents, teachers, luminaries, scientists, and specialists in every field. And we have the inner authority of our own experience—our fixed ideas based on past hurts, successes, failures, and pleasures. With this accumulated, unwieldy authority we meet the infinite mysteries of life. It is a woefully inadequate meeting.

Why do we seek out authority? Perhaps it is because we do not see the reality of life that lies before our eyes. If we saw the truth of our own natures, and the nature of the world, then our actions would be spontaneous and natural. But because we are constantly trying to escape from reality, we must have authority in order to respond to life. Response based on authority is imitation. It is not living.

Authority, either our own or that of others, is an escape from the difficult process of discovery. It is a false security, a straw to which we cling. Authority is the death of discovery. It is an end, and discovery is endless.

Truth

Is there an absolute truth, a fundamental reality that is capable of being perceived, or is all truth relative? If truth is relative then it is individualistic—something that is filtered through our individual prejudices and limited by our sense inputs—and it is therefore fragmentary, tainted, and incomplete. So can it be the truth? Something that is incomplete or twisted by our prejudices is obviously less than the truth. Yet all our knowledge, by definition, is fragmentary and tainted by bias. The known by its very nature is relative and therefore limited. So if an absolute truth exists, it must exist beyond the scope of knowledge.

$\mathcal{J}$f you watch the process of perception in yourself, you find that every experience, act, and sensation that comes to your awareness is first filtered through the background of your own conditioning. Experience is interpreted as it happens, and our interpretations are based on our unique system of beliefs, fears, cravings, and anticipations, and on our experiences in similar situations. We cannot come to the truth until we see our conditioning and dissolve it.

We may think that only the paranoid or unbalanced have twisted perceptions, but we would be wrong. All of us are a bundle of opinions, beliefs, and ideals that tell us what is "true" in people's intents; we overflow with fears and suspicions that tell us the "truth" of people's actions; we are full of pride and self-importance that tell us the "truth" of our own being.

Must we forever struggle blindly in the field of our own and others' deceptions, or is there not some absolute truth, some reality that exists independent of our past conditioning, which can be discovered? I say unconditionally that there is, and that it is hidden in the mirror of our existing relationship to the world.